TO GOD BE THE GLORY

TO GOD BE THE GLORY

A Collection of Poems Honoring The Almighty God, My Lord and Savior Jesus Christ and the Holy Spirit

LaReine A. Miller

iUniverse, Inc.

New York Lincoln Shanghai

TO GOD BE THE GLORY

A Collection of Poems Honoring The Almighty God, My Lord and Savior
Jesus Christ and the Holy Spirit

iUniverse books may be ordered through booksellers or by contacting:

iUniverse
2021 Pine Lake Road, Suite 100
Lincoln, NE 68512
www.iuniverse.com
1-800-Authors (1-800-288-4677)

Because of the dynamic nature of the Internet, any Web addresses
or links contained in this book may have changed
since publication and may no longer be valid.

ISBN: 978-0-595-43223-3 (pbk)
ISBN: 978-0-595-87564-1 (ebk)

Printed in the United States of America

CONTENTS

PREFACE

To God Be The Glory is my tribute to the Heavenly Father who has granted me the gift of poetic inspiration—a gift I cherish dearly. I had to stop last year and ask God how He wanted me to use this gift. He answered me by allowing me to create 15 poems in 11 days that I was expected to share with others—which, of course, I did. Without this gift, I could not share with you what a few have had an opportunity to read. Thank You, Lord God.

The poems contained in this volume were written as thoughts of God's goodness and mercy, His love and compassion, and His overwhelming grace were made evident to me through my life or the lives of people He brought my way. I would be remiss not to give Him the glory. I can never thank Him enough for the blessing that He has allowed my words to be for the people these poems were presented to or with whom I was allowed to share them.

ACKNOWLEDGMENTS

A few of these poems have only been seen by a select group of people who share my love for God and occasionally praise Him with me in prayer or at times when life has brought special situations in the way of one or more of us. My prayer partners, Rosenna Barnes, Augustine Edmonds, Marjorie Gorham and Pearl West; my fellow poet and sister, Gerrie Keyes; Michiele Bryant, Marie Barfield, Wilma Smith, Barbara O'Neal, Janine Benton, and Etlena Shaw, who have encouraged me continually to publish my works; my fellow workers, Catherine Johnson, Valerie Walton, Yvonne Grier, Carolyn Meredith, Monica Gainey, Rikki Redfern, Daphne Gomez, Rose Marshall (who occasionally have acted as editors)—I thank you all for your support and love. I must also acknowledge my instructor at Trinity College for Women, Lori Shpunt, whose comments and critiques are greatly appreciated.

To my mother, Mary B. Johnson (the love of my life), my sisters Norma Legette and Maria Johnson, and my children, Andréa LaReine Miller, Lillian and Richard Sylvester, Yvette and Brian Bishop, Sr., Ava Miller, Evelyn Abdelaziz and Lynne Connerton—without your love and zest for life, I would have been lost. I must also acknowledge the families of my new sons, the Blunts, Bishops and Sylvesters who are inspirations in themselves. And last, but not least, my two grandsons—Brian Ivy Bishop, Jr. and Dempsé LaReintz Sylvester—the joys of my life.

A special thanks has been sent in prayer to my father, LaReintz Anthony Johnson, Sr., who departed this life on July 20, 1997 after a long illness. He and my mother were the subjects of many of my poems that were written about parents—knowing how I feel about them often helped to provide the essence needed to express my thoughts.

I love you all and appreciate your confidence and support.—2/98—

*   *   *   *

DEDICATION

The tribute above was written for the original publication, which, though copyrighted in 1998, did not occur as planned. My mother, Mary B. Johnson, joined my father in glory in April 2005 and is sorely missed. I must state for the record that my co-worker and friend, Catherine Johnson, has been my main critic and proofreader over the years, and I appreciate her finding the flaws that I would have otherwise missed. My children, their spouses and my grandchildren continue to inspire me. My sister, Norma Faye Legette, and my long-time friends and confidantes—Michelle Bryant, Eleanor Short and Vee Williams Garcia— have been loyal supporters of my work. Thank you to all persons who have loved me through the trying times of my life which have finally resulted in completion of this work.

And I cannot close without expressing my thanks to my pastor and friend, Rev. Robert J. Williams, Sr. and his wife Lillie, for their encouragement to strengthen my relationship with God through Christ and to continue my growth in ministry through verse.

2/2008

THE MOST PRECIOUS GIFT

The most wonderful gift that this world has received
Is more precious than silver and gold;
It outshines the brightest diamonds and gems;
It's priceless—heaven knows.

All the wonders that this world beheld long ago
Can't measure up in any way
To this gift that was given one glorious morn—
Nestled in a manger of hay.

This gift was small and perfect.
A blessing for all whom God beckoned to see—
Wisemen who traveled from strange, distant lands;
And shepherds tending their sheep.

God must have looked at this world
With love and pride … and yet with sadness, too;
For the life of the Son that He gave to mankind,
Would be sacrificed for me and you.

Look with joy upon each Christmas season!
Be thankful for God's gift to man!
For if God had not loved this world so much,
Christ would not have died for our Sin.

GOD'S GIFT OF LOVE

Would you be willing to give up a child
To save the souls of others?
Would you let Him grow into a man …
Be put to death like a sheep to slaughter?

Would you allow the race from which He came
To turn their backs on Him?
Would you watch as the world used His gifts
And later mocked and crucified him?

Would you stand and let an angry mob
Condemn him to death with scorn?
Would you let the keepers of your home
Close your own doors to your child?

Think about it! That's what God allowed
When He sent this world His infant Son.
He gave His Son, Jesus, to save this world—
A world filled with sin and shame.

He watched as the young child aged and grew
Into a man who was meek and mild,
Knowing that the Son He loved so much
Would die in a little while.

God must have smiled at the infant birth!
Swelled with pride at His Son in the temple!
Felt pleased as He witnessed Jesus' wondrous works.
And held fast to complete His life's purpose.

He must have bent His head with shame
At the way that ungrateful men

Caused His grown Son to be accused and sentenced
For the wrongs of another man.

God must have wept such bitter tears
When on a cross His Son was nailed.
And once Christ gave up His life to Him
God's anger was furiously unfurled.

But imagine the glory and honor God felt
When on the third day His Son 'rose again!
When the life of the Child that He loved so much
Conquered death to redeem man from Sin!

No greater gift of love, I feel,
Will this unworthy place ever know
Than the love that God gave to this sin-sick world—
Christ's Life to save mankind's souls.

MY WALK

Lord, please let my walk daily draw me
closer still to Thee;
Let my mouth speak testimonies of Your love;
Let each situation that I face
yield sure and true report,
As I show through actions that
I do what I ought.

Touch my lips with coals of fire
That cleanse each and every word;
Fill my mind with thoughts that You'd approve.
Even when my soul's in pain,
Let me be an instrument for You
By doing the things You'd have me do.

Lord, work in me; mold me; teach me;
Help me understand Your Word;
Let me seek the Holy Spirit for direction;
May my life profess through works and deeds
That I'm a steward of Your church;
And that Christ is working through my life and in me.

GLORY TO GOD

"Glory to God in the highest!"
The angels sang that day.
"The Son of God is now on earth.
The world is His to save."

"Immanuel (God with us),"
Isaiah had proclaimed,
Would carry the weight of all the world
And shoulder the bulk of its shame.

The sins of man Christ came to clear
By shedding His precious blood;
But His greatest triumph was over the grave
To redeem us from sin with His love.

Rejoice, for God has blessed the world
With the birth of His Only Son,
Who would show us how to come back to God,
For God gave man His Son—with love.

TOUCHED BY THE HAND OF GOD

The day that God blessed this worthless world
Was the day the Lord Jesus was born.
On this day mankind received a reprieve
From sin it had lived with so long.

The heavens rejoiced at the news of His birth,
And the angels sang loudly their praise;
The lowly shepherds in the field
Had the privilege of knowing His name.

The Holy Child lay in a fresh bed of hay,
Placed in a manger that fed the farm beasts;
And the glory that must have glowed from His being
Filled the souls of all who came to see.

Behold, the Lamb of God is born!
Behold, God's Son is here!
His birth had been proclaimed long ago.
Now the Messiah had truly appeared.

God honored His Son with a wondrous star
That was seen throughout the world.
Three kings had journeyed from countries afar
To witness our dear Savior's birth.

HOLY FIRE

God's fire is burning within me;
It consumes my very soul;
For the wonders of God's blessings
Are truly more than I can contain.

He puts His loving arms around me;
His love burns within my heart;
And when I've failed to thank Him,
I feel my fire going out.

God has sent us the love of His Spirit
To fill our hearts and minds;
And the gift of His only Son, Jesus,
Has let us feel God's love divine.

O' fire from the Father,
Always dwell within my soul;
And keep me ever, ever aware
Of God's unchanging love.

Inspired by the sermon by Dr. Suzan D. Johnson-Cook, Burn, Baby, Burn! during the Women's Churchwide Revival at St. Paul Baptist Church, Capitol Heights, MD, on the evening of June 19, 1996.

DO YOU THANK GOD?

How do you thank God for His blessings?
Do you let Him know that you even care
That He has granted your heart's desire;
That He has answered a desperate prayer?

Do you stop for a moment to say, "Thank you, Lord,"
As soon as you're aware of your blessing?
Do you take the time to reflect on God's love
And praise Him without His asking?

Sometimes we are so busy looking
For the answers to our pleas;
And once received, we forget to stop
And say a silent "thank you, Lord" prayer.

Don't take God's blessings for granted,
For that blessing may be your last;
Close your eyes in silence and meditate;
Take time to tell your God, "Thanks."

PEACE

To be embraced by Jesus,
To feel arms of sweet release,
Would provide one's soul with gladness
And a true feeling of love and peace.

To be able to draw near Him
Leaving behind all woes and cares
Would allow one a sense of solace
For all your burdens He wants to share.

MISSED BLESSINGS

How many blessings have I missed
Because I failed to do Your will?
Or I failed to go where You wanted me;
Or didn't go when You wanted me to?
How much have I lost because of my faults
Through mistakes—or errors in deeds?
When I've failed to measure up to Your standards,
Because I'm looking out for my own needs?

When I have taken time to listen
To what You have told me to do,
I know that I have been blessed two-fold
For I've obeyed His command.
Why don't you do so, too!

GOD'S TEMPLE

A life is very precious;
But even we don't stop to care
About the living temple
That God gave us each to wear.
Often we abuse our bodies
Not eating healthy as we should.
Some persons seek a means of escape
By consuming alcohol or drugs.

Your body is God's temple,
And to show Him our concern we share,
We must find time to honor it
With tender loving care.

HOW MANY TIMES HAS GOD CALLED YOU?

How many times has God called you,
Begging for your listening ear;
And you, in your constant daily race,
Won't even stop to hear?

How many times has God spoken
And you failed to know His voice;
For you're so busy working
That you don't make Him your choice?

How many times has God sought you out
And you don't have time to stop;
For the world is your priority
And the Lord God is not?

Take time out to spend a moment
Throughout your busy day
To harken to the voice of God
And stop and spend time to pray.

Remember, the time you might neglect Him
Could surely be your last;
For no one is promised tomorrow
So don't let this next minute go past.

SHARING, CARING

Sometimes our hearts are filled with fear
When life deals its crushing blows,
And the weight of all that's happened
Pulls us down.
We choose to draw within ourselves
And close the world away;
We hope that others will not see
The pain that lies within.

But others often are aware
That something may be wrong.
And though we may not want to share
The burdens in our souls,
They, too, may feel the worry and the pain.

Some things we lock within our hearts
Afraid that others will know
The private hurts and sorrows
That are tormenting our souls.

But know in your heart, dear friend,
That someone else does feel your pain
And someone else is willing to share your woes.
For sometimes it helps to know
That there's someone around who cares.
Please know that you have a friend
Who'll go to God, through Christ, in prayer.

GOD'S CANVAS

The majesty of the Father can be seen
in His beautiful skies.
The canvas that's ever changing ...
the colors no artist can buy.

The hues that God lets us witness
are unlike any that man can create;
Even on an artist's palette or
on painted surface plate.

The brilliance of the sun above or
the softness of evening moonlight
Enhance the colors of the clouds and
bring still-life fireworks to the sky.

The reds, the pinks, the oranges, and
the yellows, too,
The various shades of purple are colors
that streak across skies of blue.

The brush strokes that the Father
sends show varied shapes and forms
That are forever changing with the clouds
as the earth moves ever on.

Take time to stop and marvel at the beauty
of God's skies,
And enjoy the wondrous splendor of
God's canvas that's on high.

A PLACE TO PRAY

I needed to find a place to pray,
And thought that I would go
To the church that was just
A few blocks from my job
But the doors were locked. Oh, no!

I needed to find a place to pray,
And found no church was there;
And only for a moment
Was my heart filled with despair.

I needed to find a place to pray,
And gladness was mine to behold;
"Go to the lot overlooking the bridge"
A small voice said,
"And find peace for your troubled soul."

I walked calmly to that very spot
And joy quickly filled my soul;
For I found a chapel—
Earth, sky, and trees—
A prayer haven to which I can go.

In this chapel of simplicity,
I was able to speak to the Lord;
And the peace that overcame my heart
Is a peace that I had never known,
For God's spirit was surely there.

Thank you, Father, for this world
The world we often take for granted,
Because the love You have for all who lives
Is visible in the beauty of this planet.

HE DOESN'T LEAVE US ALONE

God doesn't leave His children helpless
When trouble fills their lives.
Please know He is ever with us
In our trials and our plights!

God has always shown He's with us,
When we don't even think He cares;
But when we take time to call on Him,
He's there to answer prayer.

Put your trust in God—know He's with you!
And with those you love and cherish, too!
He will make the situation turn,
For the bad can be changed to good!

God has not left the angry
And those who turned their faces from Him,
For His hand is always open,
And His heart and love are always there to extend.

But sometimes we must be broken down
Into pieces so finite,
That only God can mend them—
Remake the pottery—set their lives right.

Let God go and believe He is with the ones
Whose souls we fear are lost—
Let God do the work that He does best—
Reclaim their lives—to <u>Him</u> they are worth the cost.

FIRST

God gives us no more to handle
Than He knows that we can bear;
If we keep our faces turned to Him,
He'll answer our every prayer.

He knows that you are human—
Filled with many fears and doubts—
For He has taught us in His Word,
Trust <u>Him</u>—shut Satan out.

Don't let your trials and sorrows
Bury you under loads of care;
Put your faith in God through Jesus <u>first</u>—
You'll find peace and solace there.

Call on the Holy Spirit
To keep emotions always in check!
Call on Him <u>before</u> you let Satan
Put His hands into the mess.

For if you will just remember—
Trust God <u>first</u> when you're oppressed—
The Spirit will fill your soul with peace,
And <u>God</u> will straighten out your mess.

GOD IS UNIVERSAL

God is universal …
No matter by what name He's known.
All of us can enter into His midst
When in secret to Him we must go.

God is universal …
Only man has created sects
For we have determined how we'll worship Him
But He's open to any who ask.

God is universal …
He'll answer every prayer;
Believe that He has heard your wants
And you'll soon receive His response to your care.

God is universal …
Take all that's important to Him;
For He'll open the gates of heaven
To all those whose souls let Him come in.

Remember, God hears every prayer one prays
If spoken in sincerity;
And He'll listen to every petition
If you show in Him you truly believe.

LET NOT YOUR HEART BE TROUBLED

Let not your heart be troubled,
If ye believe in me, He said,
I will carry all your burdens
And lift your ever pending dread.

Let not your heart be troubled,
If you abide in me, He spoke,
The Lord God is ever present
And love through me He will invoke.

Let not your heart be troubled,
For He said He would be near
To listen to your problems
And to calm your nagging fears.

Let not your heart be troubled,
For if you will just believe
You will find that God will lift your load
And give you space in which to breath.

Let not your heart be troubled,
For it is Christ, not lowly man,
Who will shoulder all your burdens
If you unload them in His hands.

Let not your heart be troubled,
For in spite of all your pain,
He will calm the world around you
And lasting peace you will attain.

Believe that God is there for you;
Ask Christ to share your load,
And in spite of the weariness you feel
God's love will soothe your tortured soul.

A LIFE FREELY GIVEN

The world fears the thought of the Holy One
Who will come to reclaim His throne;
For the evil one who rules over the earth
Knows that his reign here will be no more.

God granted mankind His most precious gift—
The birth, life, death and rise of His Son.
He allowed Jesus Christ to live and die
So from sin He could save us all.

God allowed His Son unlimited power
That He could call at His demand;
But Jesus sacrificed Himself in death
So that He could rise again.

If it had not been for Christ shedding His blood,
Mankind would not be free
To seek the mercy and the love of God
Through Christ's death on Calvary.

But death could not hold the Son of God;
And life was His again to gain;
He rose to liberate our souls.
Life eternal became our choice to claim.

We now can choose to live for God
Or to live for the evils of man;
For the sacrifice of God's Only Son,
Redeems those who heeds God's commands.

Open your hearts and souls to Christ.
When He beckons, heed His call.
For we know not the day or hour
When He'll call God's children home.

NO BOUNDARIES

God's love has no boundaries;
It is not confined by walls.
For when you find you need Him most,
He's there to answer your call.

He wants mankind to love Him
And learn to trust His Word;
For He made us to be His companions
And He wants us to seek His grace.

Especially in times of trouble
When you have no place to go;
When your back is against the wall
And your problems consume your soul—

Let not your heart be troubled!
Let Jesus come into your soul!
He'll heal the hurt that fills your life.
His love will make you whole.

Just call on the name, "Lord Jesus."
Confess your sins to Him and believe
He'll intercede on your behalf,
And God, the Father, will hear your plea.

But be careful—don't make Him promises
In your heart you know that you can't keep;
Because His wrath can be as great
As His mercy can be deep.

He wants you to know that He loves you,
And His doors are open just for you.
Even when there seems to be no way out,
God's love will see you through.

A LITTLE WHILE

A little while we're here on earth.
A little while this world we share.
And what we do with the lives we're given
Affect others whose burdens we bear.

A little while we live a borrowed life
That will never be ours to claim;
A little while we must grow and live
In a world where we leave only a name.

We come here with only our bodies,
And we leave here the same way we came;
We can't take anything with us
Not even our claims to fame.

God let us live upon this earth
For just a little while, my friend.
Don't you think it's time to consider
How to be nice to your fellow man?

None of us has a monopoly on life,
No one is better than his brother;
For all of us come here the self-same way
And leave this world just like each other.

Inspired by the message of Barbara Williams Skinner during the Women's Ministry Brunch at St. Paul Baptist Church, Capitol Heights, MD, on the afternoon of June 22, 1996.

WHAT DO I KNOW ABOUT MY GOD?

What do I know about You, God;
What do You mean to me?
When I've failed to spend my time with You,
Why do You hide from Me?

When I've thought that You've been with me
And my world is about to fall,
Why don't you ever answer
When in prayer to You I call?

I thought You'd always be beside me!
I thought You knew my name!
Why is it You don't know me
When I call out in my pain?

God's answers were very simple:
"Child, when last did you talk to me?
When did you spend some time in prayer?
When did you My wisdom seek?"

The only time you know Me
Is when your life is caving in.
Take time, instead, to read My Word and pray,
And learn to know Me as your Friend."

LIFE IS VERY PRECIOUS

Sometimes a life is taken
And we can't see the reason why.
Sometimes it's a fault of humanness
Or the body feels it has to die.
Sometimes we're left here questioning
Why God could let this be—
But only He has the answer …
The answer we'll never know or see.

Sometimes we see each other
And let feelings split our lives;
We live within our "holy" worlds
Filled with vanity and pride.
Anger, hurt and thoughtless actions
Often push families to the brink
But think about it—God forgave us.
We can forgive, too.
Stop and think.

But when families are filled with love
And someone we've loved has been lost,
We must gather in each others arms
And express our pain and loss.
We must remember all the happy times
And forgive moments that were bad
And appreciate the others who are left
Noting that this life is all we have.

Love each other as you grieve about your loss.
Smile and think that though he's gone,
God has now claimed his soul in glory
And he now lives in heaven's home.

Remember, we are only promised
One moment at a time,
And when death comes here to claim our souls
Not one of us will be left behind.

LET GO AND LET GOD HELP YOU

I can't be there to hold you
and wipe away your tears
I can't be there to hear your cries
which no one else can hear,
I can't be there to comfort you in
your moments of despair,
But I can offer up your name and problems
To our Lord Jesus Christ in prayer.

You have weighed so very heavy
On my heart and soul these days
'Til the very thought of your despair
Brings instant prayers your way.
And although you cannot hear them,
Jesus does and will obey
Your cries for inner peace and freedom
Once you let Him in to stay.

Dear one, I know that it's very hard
To let our Savior in your life,
To let go and let God handle all your miseries and strife,
But please know that He is there for you
And is waiting for your call;
The call that truly says to Him,
"Lord, I now must give You my all."

"Lord Jesus, please take all these pains
and handle them today.
Please release the pressures of my heart,
I can't take more any way,
Lord, I am coming to you because I must

surrender all
Because I am losing all control
So on your sweet name I must call."

Please listen, child of misery,
There's not much more that you can do.
You can't solve all problems that surround you
No matter what you try to do.
It's time to truly let them go,
Let God handle what is left,
Stop beating yourself into the ground
About things that are so hard to forget.

Please listen, my dear loved one,
God is waiting for your call.
Let His Son hear your total anguish,
Let Him to The Father call.
Jesus will offer your petition to
our Heavenly Father above,
But you must truly let these matters go
And let God handle them with His love.

LONELINESS

Loneliness often fills our life with fears;
Fears that we often can't shake.
And sometimes we let our souls wallow
In the feelings that help seal our fate.

We feel the world is closing in,
That no one else knows about our pain;
And instead of seeking a way to climb out
We dig our pit ever deeper each day.

We are grateful to know that others care
And recognize that we're in pain;
But instead of letting them help us out
We close our inner door again.

Loneliness helps to exaggerate
The physical hurts that our bodies feel;
And we shut ourselves into a closet
Where no light is allowed to come through.

But there is light that's shining all around us
If we'd only let it in;
And accept the love that others give
And allow that love to heal our fears.

Know that God loves you very much,
He knows the pain you feel;
But you must open up your heart
And let His love shine in.

Sometimes opening the door isn't easy,
But you must believe that God loves you;
Just open up a window in your soul
And let God's love lead you through.

Suicide has claimed the lives of young and not so young. It is staggering to realize that the stress man has placed on his world is even suffocating the lives of teenagers who should be enjoying their lives, not taking their lives.

WHEN HOPE IS GONE

When Hope becomes a stranger that you dare
not care to meet;
When you find that you can't face him on your own;
When no matter what you're doing seems
to hit you in the face,
And fear keeps you from finding open doors....

When you've tried and tried to do your best
To find a window to break through,
Yet each window is blocked with a darkened screen;
And though your eyes are open, only blackness do you see,
And light that once surrounded you dims in your soul....

"Oh, Lord God, where are You? I cannot find my way!
I don't know if I should turn left or right.
I have my hands stretched out before me,
Yet my path leads me to no where;
I am frozen in my tracks.
WHERE IS MY LIGHT?

Around you now is silence,
Except for sobs and tears you've shed;
And all the walls around you are closing in.
Since there's no path for you to walk on,
Now's the time you should STAND STILL.
STOP in your tracks!
FALL on your knees!
And PRAISE the Lord!

Praise the Lord, for He's almighty!
Praise Him!
He's worthy of <u>all</u> praise!

Give Him respect and honor that He's due!
Take time out now to thank Him for another day.
And for the many blessings that He's given you.

Ask Him for His forgiveness for the wrongs
that you have done;
Whether they were done knowingly or unknown.
Be aware you're one of many;
But all are equal in God's sight.
Ask Him for this one moment,
"BE MINE ALONE!"

Let Him know now that your path is blocked;
The light that led you is now dim;
Let Him know that you feel trapped and no where to go.
Let Him know the thoughts that burden you.
Spill out your heart and soul to Him!
Cry out, "Lord God, please help me!
Save my soul!"

Let yourself go! Call out to Him!
Shed the tears you must release!
Let the troubles that are binding you come forth.
Don't hold back! Just tell God everything!
Let words pour out!
Keep nothing hid!
Open your soul! Lay bare your heart before Him!

For He knows what you've been doing;
He knows what you're going through.
LEVEL WITH HIM!
REPENT! CONFESS! PRAY!
Remember that the life you're living
Belongs to Him and Him alone.

IT IS BORROWED!
ONCE LIFE ENDS, IT'S GOD'S TO CLAIM!

Recognize the life He's given you is no more
than you can bare;
Let Him know that you can't make it without Him.
Ask Him to guide—direct your steps;
Ask Him to show you the way—
The way your feeble life should take
—the path close to Him.

Cry out until the tears you cry can no longer flow;
Once they've stopped …
Give yourself time to take control.
Calm your spirit!
Quiet your body!
Just "be still and know"
That your prayers have reached
The Father on His Throne.

You must be still so you can learn that
HE IS GOD!
Relax! Believe that He has heard your plea!
Leave all your cares and worries
on the steps at Heavens doors.
Remember God's time is not ours …
Time belongs to Him.

BELIEVE IN HIM!
LET HIM SHOW YOU THAT HE IS GOD!
Don't snatch back problems
that you said you gave to Him.
STOP!
Remind yourself,

"They're Yours now, Lord," and then go on.
He will fight your battles
If you leave them with Him.

When you must regain your balance,
And tire of stumbling along the way,
When that stranger Hope cannot be found;
Take the time to STOP!
RELAX! AND PRAY!
SEEK INNER QUIET FOR YOUR SOUL.
For in this peace,
You'll hear the *quiet voice of God!*

This poem is dedicated to the memory of my cousin
Philip Stanley Davis
and others who find life slipping away from their grasp.

YOU'RE NOT ALONE

I don't know why God puts us
Through the trials and tests we face.
I just know that if we trust Him
He'll help us to win our race.

Sometimes the road is painful
And its burdens weigh us down;
But the load we bear is nothing
Compared to thorns in another man's crown.

Cry out in prayer—*Lord, help me!*
When you feel you're on your own.
Stop! Read His words of wisdom.
Ask Christ to help you—you're not alone.

Read your Holy Bible.
Rely on its words of truth.
God inspired men to write this manual of Life—
Mankind's spiritual textbook.

You'll find in it words of comfort and strength
That'll help you day by day
As you meet challenges of each moment,
Traveling along this earthly way.

Know that others are praying for you.
Remember—though your own tears you must shed,
There are those who have grown to love you.
They'll not forsake you. They'll also be there.

May God soon smile down you on both of you,
And fill your hearts with love, comfort and ease.
May He grant your soul strength and wisdom.
Relieve your suffering. Grant your spirits peace.

HOPE LIVES IN ME

What do I do when all seems to be lost?
What to me can I possibly say?
What is left for me to reach for
When my life seems to be wasting away?

When all seems hopeless around me
And there seems to be nowhere to go,
What words can I possibly tell myself that
Life is still mine if I believe that it's so?

What will make me know that all's not lost
And that there's still some time ahead,
When this worn, beaten, tired body of mine
Must pull itself off of my bed?

Is there anyway I can influence my mind
To convince me that I can go on?
What means of inspiration
Will fill my heart and soul with song?

King David said in Psalm One Twenty-One
To lift up my eyes to the hills for my help
For even though my body is tired
God has not left me by myself.

If I remember when problems are weighing me down
And my body's racked with aches and pain,
God has given me enough strength to wake up and rise
And stand on my own two feet once again.

All is not lost as long as I know
That my strength comes from almighty God.
I must make each day the first day of the rest of my life
For life is mine until God calls me home.

For I have family and friends who love me.
And a home in which to live;
Food on my table, clothes to wear
And a mind that's alert still.

If I think of the things God's given me
And stop feeling sorry for myself,
Perhaps I can be a blessing
And share my skills with someone else.

Thank You, heavenly Father,
For giving me one more day.
Is there a way I can help someone else?
Show me how to bless someone this day.

I'm still able to do what I have to do
To function for and by myself;
But I must believe that each day is mine to claim
And share part of it with someone else.

The next poem, AN IMMORTAL, ENDEARING LOVE, was inspired by the message delivered by REV. DESIREE GROGRAN at the Women's Ministry's 11 a.m. service, Sunday, June 23, 1996 at St. Paul Baptist Church, Capitol Heights, MD.

AN IMMORTAL, ENDEARING LOVE

Is my soul truly anchored
In the love of Jesus Christ?
Have I allowed myself to be prepared?
When time comes to pay the price
For the gift of His salvation
Through the spilling of His blood,
And the nailing of His out-stretched Hands
And His sacrifice of love?

Am I truly open to service
In the way He needs me most?
Do my actions truly proclaim louder
Than my uttered boasts?
Am I freely working for Him,
Giving Him my all and all?
Will I be awake and ready
To answer My Master's call?

Lord, daily I am striving
To be worthy of Your love;
To help those You've sent who need me;
To minister to those I know are lost.
You have blessed my life so openly;
You haven't spared a bit.
For when I think my cup is empty
I find it spilling from its brim!

Lord, let my life be a testimony
Of the blood You've shed for me;
Let my heart and soul be mindful
Of what You would have me be.
Let me truly be an instrument
Of Your Immortal, Endearing Love;
Let my actions show in all I do that
"Yes, child, you're worthy of My Love."

A SHEPHERD'S TALK WITH HIS LORD AND GOD

"I'm only a man, Lord," I heard him say
As he knelt beside his bed;
"I'm trying to do the best that I can
To live my life Your way.

I've faced all manner of temptations
And I suffered long for my mistakes
But I've learned that I can come back to You
No matter how often I stray.

"I'm tired, Lord. I've been working so long
To do the things that You want me to do.
There are times that I've felt pushed and pulled
And sometimes close to being abused.

I daily and faithfully read Your word
To learn the things I ought
And I find many times throughout the day
That I must kneel to You in prayer and talk.

"Lord, what would You have me do for You
That I have failed to do?
How can I lead Your people, Lord,
To bring them closer still to You?
What more must I teach them, dear Jesus,
That will last their whole life through?

"I trust that in my daily life
I show them by my example
That I have learned to trust in You
And I'm willing to be a living sample

Of a man who can walk upright with God
And profess through mouth and deed
Of the goodness and mercy of Your love
And the blessing of being redeemed.

"Thank you, dear Lord, for showing me
Through your life and sacrifice
How a shepherd must daily lead his flock
In spite of toil and strife.
And how, regardless of the pain,
He puts his safety and feelings last
In order to make a safe escape
For the sheep that must still get past.

"It's the shepherd's job to guide and to protect
And keep his flock from harm
But it's nice to know that even he can find
Lasting shelter in Your loving arms.

"Continue to be my guide, dear Lord,
As I struggle each day to live
The life that every good Christian ought
As long as there's breath in me to give.
I hope that I teach my loving flock
That each one's heart and soul is Yours
And that they, too, must work daily to protect
The ones that they love and adore.

May I continue to show them the way to You
As I minister through Your Word and teach
The lessons that I've found to be true
And pray young and old my words do reach.
And I pray that the meanings of life as You've taught
Will guide me my whole life through

So that when my days have finally ended
My crown I'll have earned
For the battle I've fought for you."

This poem is dedicated to my father, REV. LAREINTZ A. JOHNSON, SR., and all men and women who have devoted their lives to serving God through our Lord and Savior Jesus Christ.

THE POTTER AND HIS CLAY

The Potter's wheel is turning …
Molding this sad, gray lump of clay.
In spite of all His efforts,
He must stop—then start again.

It seems at times He's succeeded
To make this mass something nice;
But then He finds a crack or hole …
Puts it down—then starts from scratch.

Once He seems happy with the shape He's made,
It's placed into an oven of flame …
Baked once more—then out it comes.
Cooled off—then stored away.

He takes it down another day
And finds the pot again is cracked.
Lovingly, He holds it in His hands—
This spot, too, He must mend.

The pot is taken and reshaped
Until again He thinks it's right—
Then back it goes into the oven of fire—
Trapped once more—door shut tight—more pain.

God is the Potter into whose hands
He's taken this limp, sad lump of clay.
He's molded and reshaped this hapless soul
Over and over again.

He is so careful to shape this vessel
Into a beautiful, loving soul.
He wants me perfect   ever ready
So I am able to fulfill His will.

MY CHILD, YES, YOU DO MATTER

In the days that have now passed me,
Days that often were filled with tears,
I look back and often wonder
How I managed to still be here.

I have felt so often lonely
Believing no one on earth really cared
About the troubles that beset my soul
And the sorrows I had to bear.

Dear Father, up in Your heaven,
Why have you left me here alone
To deal with all these heartaches
That torment my weary soul?

Why, God, must I feel so much pain
And long for sweet release
Knowing that each day is a struggle
And each is harder still to reach?

But, "Why?," my soul does cry out,
"Must I bear this cross alone?
Why do I feel discouraged?
How can I face this day again alone?"

But a voice within me answers,
"Child, you're not by yourself
I have always been here for you
Only me, and no one else.

I have never once forsaken you
Though alone you may often feel
For I've been right here beside you;
All you had to do was hear.

I love you, child of loneliness,
I have often felt your woe.
I have heard you cry your tears at night;
I have seen your sorrow grow.

Child, don't you know that you do matter?
Don't you know I love you so?
Can't you feel my love around you?
Can't you hear my voice so low?

Remember—I've sent others to you
Who love you and feel your pain?
When they tried to console you,
You wouldn't let them near?

Baby, I have never left you,
I would never let you go.
I have been here waiting for you
To let me into your soul once more.

You've forgotten me, my child,
But I have never forgotten you,
Come back within my bosom
Love me like you used to do.

Read again my Words of wisdom;
Read the book written just for you,
With Words that teach you how to live,
And find the faith that you once knew.

Learn again about my love for you
Despite the heartaches and the pain;

Find within their deeper meanings
Faith that will make you whole again.

Yes, my child, you do matter.
You mean oh so much to me;
But you must believe within yourself
The love I give you can redeem.

You are ever so important,
You have shared your love so sweet,
Don't you know that others notice?
They've tried to give, but you won't receive.

Look within yourself, my child of woe,
Look within yourself and see
What a wonderful person you really are
How your presence is truly received.

Look within your soul, my child of grief,
You've given so much of yourself
That you've lost the one who matters most,
My child, you've lost yourself.

Look inside of your soul's mirror—
You must want to reach in deep—
Find the warmth inside that's hidden;
Find the love of self you need.

You must believe, my child, that you matter,
You must accept that you are good.
You must fight daily to find out a little more
About the person who's fled from you.

You must face each day believing
YOU are someone who really counts.

You must know within your heart of hearts
That your life's important without a doubt.

Open up, my child, please hear me—
I haven't left you all alone
Without some way to salvage
What you've lost inside your soul.

Please know, child, that I love you,
I'm here whenev'r you're ready to receive
All the joy and warmth I offer
For you are mine, but YOU must believe.

RELEASE

Take your hands off of the things that you treasure;
And release them into Jesus' hands;
Know that these are all temporary
For in death you <u>will</u> surrender them.

You may accumulate material treasures—
Money, clothing, jewels, and the like—
But you can't take these things with you
When you've reached the end of this life.

When an episode of tragedy
Has left your heart and mind in despair—
The best way to deal with the agony
Is to go to God in prayer.

Talk to Jesus about your troubles
And release your burdens and your cares;
But be careful—don't leave the altar
Reclaiming the problems you said you'd leave there.

Jesus makes time to hear your problems,
For He is always there
To listen to your deepest concerns and plights,
And to answer your most fervent prayers.

But you must willingly let go and allow Him
To handle what you've left in His hands;
Remind yourself when you're tempted to take them back,
"Lord, I left this in your care."

Let go and let Jesus help you
The way only He can do;
For 'though your problem may seem to be yours alone,
He's helping others while He's helping you.

There's a time when we all must move away
From the things that linked us to a painful past;
So be happy! Rejoice! And thank the Lord!
Trust Jesus and find true peace at last.

These two poems were written as part of our family's thank you to everyone who expressed their love and support during the passing of my father, Reverend LaReintz Anthony Johnson, Sr.,(July 20, 1997).

ONE NEVER KNOWS

One never knows when words he has spoken
May be soothing a mind filled with despair.
Sometimes even a pleasant smile
May bring light to a face filled with care.

There are even times when a friendly hug
May bring relief from trials and strain.
One may not know when being thoughtful
May be healing his fellow man.

GOD KNEW US

God knew us before we were conceived
Within our mothers' wombs.
He knew the paths that we'd choose to walk,
And lives that would cross our lives, too.
He knew before we made the choice
What roadblocks lay ahead.
Yet, any way we'd choose to go,
All roads still can lead back to Him.

SELFISHNESS

I passed a man on the streets today—
Choosing food from a corner trash can.
My lunch was held tightly in my fist as he dug,
Yet, I failed to move from the spot—bag in hand.

Hesitation showed by my very stance ...
It hurt to see him search for food.
Yet, I stood on the sidewalk watching him—
Unsure of what I should do.

He carefully placed the morsels he'd found
In the wrappings or bags that they came in.
He did not seem to notice the glances—the stares—
Or care that others were looking at him.

Silently—carefully—he finished his search;
Storing his treasure for future feasting.
He had hidden it in the cart that he pushed,
Lined with rags and other things that he needed.

Later, as I completed the meal that I'd held,
I found I had not eaten it all;
My waste would have been a feast to that soul,
Yet I'd thrown out scraps—bread, meat—all!

"Waste not! Want not!" Is what the old adage says.
Yet, how many of us take for granted
The food that we've wasted or harbored for self
Without sharing a crumb of our own lunch package?

The hesitation that's faced when we witness a scene
That perhaps we ourselves can fix,
Shows how we fail to share with others
The goodness that God to us has given.

O, Lord, please forgive my selfishness!
For the bag that I'd held in my hand
Could have spared that soul from his careful search;
Fed his need!—Was that part of Your plan?

Because of my failure to respond, did I miss out on a future blessing?
Did my selfish failure to respond cost me an angel's blessing?

Shamefully Witnessed & Written in 5/97

DAILY BLESSINGS—COUNT THEM

God's blessings are many, though often overlooked ... But sometimes you must sit down and count them.

1. God's awakened you to see a brand new day. Yesterday is gone. Live for today. The Lord will take care of tomorrow.

2. Enjoy knowing that CHRIST is your Savior and you are His child. Keep Him involved in <u>all</u> the things that you must do in this life.

3. You're able each morning to look into the eyes of the people whom you love and bask in the warmth of that feeling.

4. In spite of aches and pains, you're in very good health.

5. Your family and friends love you dearly. They may not always agree with your wisdom, but they do hear you when you speak.

6. You're admired by those who have gotten to know you.

7. If you can't see other family members, you can at least call them to hear their voices.

8. God has allowed you to reach out and work for your education. You can, and will be able to, pursue your career if you are patient and will let God open doors for you.

9. USE YOUR TIME WISELY—while you have the chance, <u>be creative</u>! Now's the time to dream up activities for the children God will give you to teach. TIME BRINGS WISDOM!!

10. You've had the privilege of being known and loved by family and loved ones who are no longer with us. Smile and know that you were special to each of them and that they're watching over you with love.

Most importantly, God's given you YOUR BIRTHDAY as the beginning of your own personal NEW YEAR—your personal anniversary. Savor it! Enjoy knowing that you are loved!

OUR HEAVENLY FATHER

OUR HEAVENLY FATHER has given each of us special gifts. Many of us choose to play around with them, but never use them to enhance His kingdom. He's given everyone of us talents that our uniquely ours. Yes, some of us can draw, sing, dance, write, cook, heal, entertain others. All of us have some God-given gift that has endeared us to someone else, even if it's nothing more than caring and taking care of one's fellow person.

Don't waste or take for granted the abilities that God has given you. For if you fail to use them for the good of this world, you will find yourself without them.

Share your gifts with others. No matter how insignificant they may appear to be to you, they may prove to be a blessing for someone else to enjoy.

God Bless!

ABOUT THE AUTHOR

God has gifted me with the ability to create poems filled with joy, comfort, and/or consolation for many people. Many of them already have been shared with those for whom they were written, and now, I am stepping forth by faith in God's grace as I share this collection of works with others. A mother and grandmother, I am a native Washingtonian (DC) who resides in nearby Maryland.

LaReine A. Miller

978-0-595-43223-3
0-595-43223-9

Printed in the United States
202389BV00003B/115-204/P